COACHING

Coaching and its importance

DELIGHT NKEM

TABLE OF CONTENT

Chapter one — 4
Introduction to Coaching
A brief overview of what coaching is and its benefits.

Chapter Two — 7
Coaching Styles
A discussion of different coaching styles and when to use them.

Chapter Three — 11
Coaching process

Chapter Four — 14
Building Trust and Rapport
The importance of building trust and rapport with your clients.

Chapter Five — 17
Active Listening and Questioning Techniques for active listening and asking powerful questions.

Chapter Six — 20
Setting Goals and Action Planning
A guide to setting goals and creating action plans with your clients.

Chapter Seven — 22
Overcoming Challenges and Obstacles

Strategies for helping clients overcome challenges and obstacles.

Chapter Eight   24
Performance Management
A discussion of performance management and how it relates to coaching.

Chapter Nine   27
Ethics and Professionalism in coaching
Importance of ethical and professional conduct in coaching.

Chapter Ten   32
Continuous Professional Development, guide to ongoing professional development for coaches.

Chapter Eleven   35
Conclusion
A summary of key takeaways from coaching.

CHAPTER ONE

INTRODUCTION TO COACHING

Coaching is a collaborative and supportive process between a coach and a client aimed at helping the client achieve their personal or professional goals. It is a relationship between two individuals in which the coach facilitates the client's growth and development by helping them obtain insight, establish and meet goals, and get over challenges.

The coaching process is built on the foundation of trust and mutual respect between the coach and client. The coach acts as a sounding board, listener, and accountability partner to the client, providing guidance and support along the way.

BENEFITS OF COACHING:

Clarity and focus: Coaching helps individuals gain clarity on their goals, priorities, and what they truly want to achieve.

Improved performance: Coaching can lead to improved performance, whether it be in the workplace or in personal life.

Increased confidence: Working with a coach can boost an individual's confidence, as they gain a deeper comprehension of their talents and qualities.

Better decision making: Coaching can help individuals make better decisions, as they are able to see the bigger picture and weigh all options before making a choice.

Personal growth: Coaching provides individuals with the opportunity for personal growth, as they are encouraged to reflect on their experiences and learn from them.

Improved relationships: By working on personal and professional goals, individuals can improve relationships with others and increase their overall satisfaction in life.

However, coaching is a valuable tool for individuals seeking to improve their personal or professional lives. It provides a supportive environment in which individuals can explore their goals, strengths, and challenges, and gain the knowledge and skills necessary to achieve success.

CHAPTER TWO

COACHING STYLES

Coaching styles refer to the different approaches and methods used by coaches to help their clients achieve their goals. There are many different coaching styles, each with its own strengths and limitations, and the most effective style often depends on the individual client and their specific needs.

Here are a few common coaching styles:

Directive coaching: Directive coaching involves the coach giving specific advice and direction to the client. This style is useful for clients who need clear guidance and direction in order to achieve their goals. In this style, the coach takes a more authoritative approach and helps the client by providing specific feedback and suggestions for improvement.

Non-directive coaching: Non-directive coaching involves the coach asking open-ended questions and allowing the client to find their own solutions. This style is useful for clients who are looking for self-discovery and personal growth. The coach takes a more facilitative approach and helps the client by encouraging them to explore their own thoughts and feelings, and to find their own solutions.

Transformational coaching: Transformational coaching is focused on helping clients make profound and lasting changes in their lives. The client and coach collaborate to investigate their values, beliefs, and motivations in order to help them make meaningful change. This style is most effective for clients who are looking to make significant changes in their lives and want to explore their inner motivations and desires.

Solution-focused coaching: Solution-focused coaching is focused on identifying and addressing the specific issues and problems that the client is facing. The client and the coach collaborate to identify practical and effective solutions to their problems. This style is most effective for clients who have specific challenges or problems that they need to overcome.

Performance coaching: Performance coaching is focused on improving specific skills and behaviors in order to enhance the client's performance. This style is useful for clients who need help with specific tasks or goals, such as public speaking or leadership. The coach helps the client by providing feedback and suggestions for improvement, and helping them to develop the skills and behaviors needed to succeed.

Moreover, each coaching style has its own strengths and limitations, and the best approach will depend on the individual client and their specific needs and goals. A skilled coach should be able to use a variety of styles as needed and adapt their approach to best meet the needs of each client.

It's important to note that these styles are not mutually exclusive and that coaches often use a combination of approaches to meet the needs of their clients.

The most effective coaching style will depend on the individual client and their specific needs and goals. The coach should work closely with the client to understand their needs and to choose the most appropriate approach to help them achieve their desired outcomes.

CHAPTER THREE

THE COACHING PROCESS

The coaching process is a structured and collaborative approach between a coach and a client to help the client achieve their desired outcomes. It typically includes the following steps:

Goal Setting: The first step in the coaching process is to establish the client's goals. The coach works with the client to clarify what they want to achieve and to set specific, measurable, and attainable goals.

Assessment: The next step is to assess the current situation and identify any obstacles that may be preventing the client from achieving their goals. This may involve reviewing the client's strengths and weaknesses, exploring past experiences and habits, and identifying areas for improvement.

Feedback: The coach provides feedback to the client on their progress towards their goals and offers suggestions for improvement. This feedback helps the client understand their strengths and weaknesses and identify areas for growth.

Action Planning: Based on the assessment and feedback, the coach and client work together to create an action plan to achieve the goals. This plan should be specific, actionable, and include steps to overcome any obstacles that were identified in the assessment.

Implementation: The client implements the action plan and the coach provides ongoing support and direction to keep the client on course.

Evaluation: Regular evaluations of the client's progress are conducted to ensure that the coaching is effective and to make any necessary adjustments to the action plan.

Reflection: The coaching process should also include opportunities for reflection, in which the client considers what they have learned, how they have grown, and what they would like to focus on in the future.

However, the coaching process is a dynamic and iterative process that helps the client achieve their desired outcomes by clarifying goals, assessing the current situation, providing feedback, creating an action plan, and monitoring progress. The coach and client work together to make adjustments as needed and to continuously improve the coaching process.

CHAPTER FOUR

BUILDING TRUST & RAPPORT

Building trust and rapport with clients is an essential aspect of any successful professional relationship, especially in fields such as sales, therapy, consulting, or coaching. Here's why:

Establishes a foundation for communication: Trust and rapport allow for open, honest, and effective communication between the client and the professional. This leads to a better understanding of the client's needs, goals, and expectations.

Increases client engagement: When clients trust and feel comfortable with their professional, they are more likely to be engaged in the process, ask questions, and provide honest feedback. This leads to a better outcome and more satisfaction for both parties.

Facilitates the development of a relationship: Building trust and rapport can lead to the development of a long-term relationship between the client and professional. This is especially important in fields where repeat business or referrals are critical to success.

Helps to establish credibility: A professional who is trusted and has good rapport with their clients is seen as credible and reliable. This can help to attract new clients and can lead to positive word-of-mouth referrals.

Creates a sense of safety: Trust and rapport help clients feel safe and secure in their relationship with their professional. This can be especially important in fields such as therapy or coaching, where clients may be sharing personal and sensitive information.

Building trust and rapport takes time and effort. It involves actively listening to clients, being transparent, and demonstrating genuine care and concern for their well-being. Consistently meeting client needs and following through on commitments can also contribute to building trust and rapport.

Building trust and rapport with clients is a critical component of any successful professional relationship. It can lead to better outcomes, increased engagement, and a more satisfying experience for both parties.

CHAPTER FIVE

ACTIVE LISTENING AND QUESTIONING

Active Listening

In order to effectively communicate, one must fully concentrate on, comprehend, and retaining information being communicated. It requires putting aside distractions and actively engaging with the speaker to comprehend the meaning behind their words and emotions.

Techniques for Active Listening:

Pay attention: Focus on the speaker, making eye contact and avoiding distractions such as your phone or other interruptions.

Show interest: Nod, smile, and use other non-verbal cues to demonstrate your interest in what the speaker is saying.

Reflect and paraphrase: Repeat back what you heard the speaker say, in your own words, to demonstrate understanding and encourage further elaboration.

Avoid interruptions: Let the speaker finish their thought before responding or asking a question.

Ask clarifying questions: If you're unsure about something the speaker has said, ask for clarification to gain a better understanding.

Empathize: Make an effort to comprehend the speaker's viewpoint and feelings.

Suspend judgment: Hold back on forming an opinion until the speaker has finished their message.

Questioning:

Asking powerful questions is an effective way to encourage deeper thinking and promote active listening. Powerful questions are open-ended and allow the speaker to explore and expand on their thoughts.

Techniques for Asking Powerful Questions:

Ask questions that can't just be answered with a simple "yes" or "no" response.

Probing questions: Follow up with additional questions to encourage the speaker to delve deeper into their thoughts and feelings.

Reflective questions: Ask the speaker to reflect on their experiences and emotions related to the topic at hand.

Challenging questions: Ask questions that challenge assumptions or encourage the speaker to think differently.

Clarifying questions: Ask questions to help the speaker clarify their thoughts and provide more information.

By using active listening and questioning techniques, individuals can improve their communication skills, deepen their understanding of others, and build stronger relationships.

CHAPTER SIX

SETTING GOALS AND ACTION PLANNING

Setting goals and action planning is a process that involves defining specific, measurable, achievable, relevant, and time-bound (SMART) goals, and creating a plan of action to achieve them. It helps clients focus on what they want to achieve, prioritize their goals, and stay on track.

Here's a guide to help you work with your clients on setting goals and creating action plans:

Identify client's goals: Ask your client what they want to achieve and what their priorities are.

Develop SMART goals: Help the client convert their goals into SMART goals by making them specific, measurable, achievable, relevant, and time-bound.

Create an action plan: Work with your client to create a step-by-step plan of action to achieve their goals. This plan should include specific tasks, deadlines, and accountability measures.

Prioritize actions: Help your client prioritize the actions in their action plan based on their importance and urgency.

Monitor progress: Regularly check in with your client to see how they're progressing and make any necessary adjustments to their action plan.

Celebrate successes: Celebrate with your client when they achieve their goals and help them set new goals to continue their progress.

By following this guide, you can help your clients achieve their goals and reach their full potential.

Chapter Seven

Overcoming Challenges: Strategies

Overcoming challenges and obstacles requires a combination of personal skills, resilience, and effective strategies.

Here are some common strategies that can help clients overcome challenges and obstacles:

Setting achievable goals: Encourage clients to set realistic and achievable goals, breaking larger goals into smaller steps.

Mindset shift: Help clients shift their mindset from a negative to a positive one, emphasizing the importance of resilience and perseverance. To develop a grit mind set.

Problem-solving skills: Teach clients effective problem-solving skills, such as analyzing the situation, generating alternative solutions, and making a plan.

Time management: Encourage clients to prioritize tasks and manage their time more effectively to reduce stress and increase efficiency.

Self-care: Emphasize the importance of self-care, such as exercise, healthy eating, and relaxation, in managing stress and maintaining overall well-being.

Seek support: Encourage clients to seek support from family, friends, or a professional when needed.

Reframing: Teach clients to reframe negative thoughts and emotions into positive ones, changing their perspective and reducing anxiety.

Adaptability: Encourage clients to embrace change and adapt to new challenges, developing a growth mindset and resilience.

It is important to remember that overcoming challenges and obstacles is a personal and unique process, and different strategies will work for different clients.

CHAPTER EIGHT

PERFORMANCE MANAGEMENT & COACHING

Performance management is a process that involves evaluating an individual's job performance and providing feedback and coaching to improve performance and achieve organizational goals.

It is a continuous process that starts with setting expectations and goals, and concludes with evaluating results and providing feedback. There are formal and informal ways to manage performance, and typically involves regular performance evaluations and coaching sessions.

The process of performance management can be broken down into several steps:

Setting expectations: This involves establishing clear goals and expectations for the individual's performance. The goals should align with the overall goals of the organization and be specific, measurable, attainable, relevant, and time-bound (SMART).

Monitoring performance: This involves ongoing observation of the individual's performance, documenting their progress and identifying areas for improvement.

Providing feedback: This involves sharing the observations and progress made by the individual, both positive and negative, and providing constructive feedback to help the individual understand their strengths and weaknesses.

Coaching: This involves working with the individual to develop and implement strategies to improve their performance. Coaching can involve providing guidance, support, and feedback to help the individual reach their goals.

Performance management and coaching are closely related, as coaching is a key component of performance management. The goal of coaching is to help the individual understand their performance and develop skills to improve their performance. Coaching can be used to address specific performance issues or to help the individual achieve specific goals.

However, performance management is a critical aspect of human resource management, as it helps organizations to achieve their goals and improve employee performance. By setting clear expectations, monitoring performance, providing feedback, and coaching, organizations can create a supportive environment that encourages growth

CHAPTER NINE

ETHICS AND PROFESSIONALISM IN COACHING

THE IMPORTANCE OF ETHICAL AND PROFESSIONAL CONDUCT IN COACHING

Ethics and professionalism are essential components of effective coaching. Coaching involves building trust and rapport with clients, and ethical and professional conduct is essential to maintaining this relationship. In addition, ethical and professional conduct is necessary to ensure that coaching practices are safe, effective, and aligned with professional standards and best practices.

Some of the key aspects of ethical and professional conduct in coaching include:

Confidentiality: Coaches must maintain the confidentiality of their clients and not disclose any information without the client's express consent, except in exceptional circumstances where when doing so is required by law or when the client or others could be harmed.

Respect for client autonomy: Coaches must respect the autonomy of their clients and not put their personal views or opinions on the customer. The client must be free to make their own decisions and take their own actions without coercion or manipulation.

Informed consent: Coaches must obtain informed consent from their clients before engaging in coaching, and ensure that clients understand the coaching process and their rights.

Competence: Coaches must have the necessary knowledge, skills, and experience to provide effective coaching. They must also continue to develop their skills and knowledge to maintain their professional competence.

Dual relationships: Coaches must avoid dual relationships with clients, such as engaging in romantic or sexual relationships, as these can compromise the coach's ability to be objective and can create conflicts of interest.

Professional standards: Coaches must adhere to professional standards and best practices in coaching, and be familiar with ethical codes and guidelines for their profession.

Professional coaching standards are a set of ethical and competency-based guidelines that aim to ensure quality and consistency in coaching practice.

Here are some of the most widely recognized professional coaching standards:

Ethical Standards: Coaches are expected to adhere to ethical standards that promote trust, transparency, and accountability in their coaching relationships. These standards typically include confidentiality, informed consent, client autonomy, and conflict of interest management.

Competency Standards: Coaches are expected to demonstrate proficiency in core coaching competencies, including active listening, powerful questioning, goal setting, and action planning. The International Coaching Federation (ICF) has identified 11 core competencies for professional coaches.

Professional Development: Coaches are expected to engage in ongoing professional development to enhance their coaching skills and knowledge. This may include attending training programs, obtaining certifications, participating in supervision or mentorship programs, and keeping up-to-date with the latest research and best practices in coaching.

Continuing Education: Coaches are expected to continue their education and stay up-to-date with the latest coaching trends and developments. This may include attending conferences, workshops, and seminars, reading industry publications, and participating in online forums and discussion groups.

Supervision: Coaches are encouraged to seek supervision or mentorship from more experienced coaches to ensure that they are providing high-quality coaching services and meeting professional standards.

Professionalism: Coaches are expected to conduct themselves in a professional and ethical manner at all times. This includes maintaining appropriate boundaries with clients, avoiding dual relationships, and adhering to legal and regulatory requirements.

The above are just some of the professional standards in coaching, and there may be variations based on different coaching organizations or countries.

Professional conduct refers to the set of standards, behaviors, and ethical principles that individuals in a profession are expected to adhere to. It encompasses the way professionals interact with clients, colleagues, and the broader society, and is intended to ensure that their work is carried out in a responsible and ethical manner.

Some key aspects of professional conduct include:

Professionalism: This involves conducting oneself in a manner that reflects positively on the profession and its values. Professionals should act with integrity, honesty, and respect, and should always strive to provide high-quality service to their clients.

Ethical behavior: Professionals should adhere to the ethical principles of their profession, which may include confidentiality, informed consent, and avoiding conflicts of interest. They should also be aware of the potential consequences of their actions and take steps to minimize harm to their clients.

Continuing education: Professionals should stay up-to-date with the latest developments in their field and engage in ongoing learning and professional development. This can help them provide better service to their clients and stay current with changes in the industry.

Accountability: Professionals should be willing to take responsibility for their actions and be accountable for the quality of their work. They should also be open to feedback and willing to make changes to improve their performance.

Overall, professional conduct is essential for building trust and maintaining the integrity of a profession. By following these standards and principles, professionals can help ensure that they are providing the best possible service to their clients and contributing to the overall well-being of society.

However, ethical and professional conduct is critical to the success of coaching and to maintaining the trust and confidence of clients. By adhering to ethical and professional standards, coaches can provide safe, effective, and respectful coaching services to their clients.

THE IMPORTANCE OF ETHICAL AND PROFESSIONAL CONDUCT IN COACHING

Ethical and professional conduct are essential in coaching for several reasons

Establishing Trust and Credibility: Ethical and professional conduct helps to build trust and credibility with clients. Clients are more likely to feel comfortable sharing personal information and goals with a coach who operates with integrity and adheres to ethical principles.

Protecting Client Confidentiality: Ethical conduct requires coaches to protect client confidentiality. This means coaches should not share or disclose any personal information about their clients without their permission, except in cases where it is necessary to prevent harm or danger to the client or others.

Maintaining Boundaries: Coaches must maintain clear boundaries between themselves and their clients to ensure that the coaching relationship remains professional and appropriate. This includes avoiding any conflicts of interest or dual relationships that could compromise the coaching relationship.

Ensuring Quality of Service: Ethical and professional conduct requires coaches to provide high-quality coaching services to their clients. This means coaches should continually develop their coaching skills, seek out feedback, and hold themselves accountable to a high standard of coaching excellence.

Upholding the Reputation of the Profession: Ethical and professional conduct helps to uphold the reputation of the coaching profession. Coaches who operate with integrity and adhere to ethical principles demonstrate that coaching is a trustworthy and reputable profession.

Ethical and professional conduct is critical in coaching because it helps to establish trust and credibility with clients, protects client confidentiality, maintains appropriate boundaries, ensures the quality of coaching services, and upholds the reputation of the coaching profession.

Chapter ten

CPD for Coaching Guide

Continuous Professional Development (CPD) refers to the ongoing process of learning and improvement that individuals undertake in order to enhance their professional knowledge, skills, and competence in their field of work. This applies to coaches as well, and is crucial to maintain high standards of professionalism and excellence in their coaching practice.

Here is a guide to continuous professional development for coaches:

Identify your learning needs: As a coach, it is essential to assess your current level of knowledge, skills, and competence, and identify areas where you would like to improve. This could be in the form of new coaching techniques, additional knowledge in a particular area, or developing new skills.

Set goals: Once you have identified your learning needs, set specific and achievable goals for your professional development. This could be attending a workshop, completing a course, or reading a certain number of books related to coaching.

Research and select learning opportunities: Research various learning opportunities available, such as workshops, conferences, online courses, or coaching certification programs. Choose opportunities that align with your goals and learning needs.

Engage in learning activities: Engage in a variety of learning activities, such as attending workshops, participating in online courses, reading relevant books and articles, and attending professional development events.

Reflect and evaluate: After each learning experience, take time to reflect on what you have learned and how it can be applied to your coaching practice. Evaluate your progress towards your professional development goals and assess if they have been met.

Keep records: Keeping records of your professional development activities, including certificates, notes, and feedback, is important for demonstrating your ongoing commitment to

CPD and your professional development.

However, continuous professional development is a crucial aspect of coaching, and enables coaches to stay up-to-date with the latest knowledge, skills, and practices in the field. By engaging in regular professional development activities, coaches can enhance their coaching practice, improve their clients' outcomes, and advance their careers

CHAPTER ELEVEN

CONCLUSION

In conclusion, here are some key takeaways from coaching:

Coaching is a process of helping individuals or teams to improve their performance and achieve their goals. It involves a structured and collaborative approach where a coach works with the client to identify their strengths and weaknesses, set goals, and create an action plan to achieve those goals.

Coaching can be used in a variety of contexts, including personal development, career development, leadership development, and sports performance. The coach uses a variety of techniques such as questioning, active listening, feedback, and goal-setting to help clients overcome challenges, build confidence, and develop new skills.

The benefits of coaching include increased self-awareness, improved communication skills, enhanced leadership abilities, increased motivation, and improved performance. Coaching can be delivered in person or virtually, and sessions may be one-on-one or in a group setting.

Self-awareness: Coaching can help you become more self-aware by identifying your strengths, weaknesses, and blind spots.

Goal setting: Setting clear and specific goals can help you focus on what you want to achieve and create a roadmap for success.

Action planning: Once you have set your goals, coaching can help you create a plan of action to achieve them.

Accountability: Having a coach to hold you accountable for your actions and progress can be a powerful motivator.

Mindset: Coaching can help you shift your mindset from a fixed mindset to a growth mindset, which can help you overcome challenges and achieve your goals.

Communication skills: Coaching can help you improve your communication skills, which can benefit you both personally and professionally.

Leadership skills: Coaching can help you develop leadership skills, which can be valuable in both your personal and professional life.

Coaching is not therapy, counseling, or consulting, as the focus is on the future and goal achievement rather than exploring past issues or providing expert advice. The coaching relationship is based on mutual trust and respect, and the coach's role is to support the client in achieving their goals while holding them accountable for their actions.

Overall, coaching can be a transformative experience that can help you achieve your goals, improve your skills, and enhance your overall well-being.